Lucy Moore works for BRF as Messy Church Team Leader. She is responsible for developing the work of Messy Church nationally and internationally—writing, speaking, reflecting and developing Messy projects. She continues to help lead the local Messy Church in her own church, where her husband is the minister.

Before working full-time with Messy Church, Lucy was a member of BRF's Barnabas children's ministry team, offering training for those wanting to bring the Bible to life for children in churches and schools across the UK, and using drama and storytelling to explore the Bible with children herself.

Her books include the *Messy Church* series, *Bethlehem Carols Unplugged*, *The Gospels Unplugged*, *The Lord's Prayer Unplugged* and *Colourful Creation* (all Barnabas) and *All-Age Worship* (BRF, 2010), and she presents the *Messy Church* DVD.

A secondary school teacher by training, she enjoys acting, walking Minnie the dog, marvelling at the alien world of her two teenage children and watching unsuitable television.

Messy Church is growing! Every month, families who have never set foot in a church before are enjoying Messy Church, and every month more Messy Churches are started all over the UK and worldwide. Messy Church is proving effective in sharing God's good news with families across denominations and church traditions. We estimate that some 100,000 people belong to Messy Churches—and the number is growing all the time. For more information about Messy Church, visit www.messychurch.org.uk.

Messy Church is enabled, resourced and supported by BRF (Bible Reading Fellowship), a Registered Charity, as one of its core ministries. BRF makes Messy Church freely available and derives no direct income from the work that we do to support it in the UK and abroad.

Would you be willing to support this ministry with your prayer and your giving? To find out more, please visit www.messychurch.org.uk/champions.

Messy Church® is a registered word mark and the logo is a registered device mark of The Bible Reading Fellowship.

Text copyright © Lucy Moore 2011
Illustrations copyright © Simon Smith 2011
The author asserts the moral right
to be identified as the author of this work

Published by
The Bible Reading Fellowship
15 The Chambers, Vineyard
Abingdon OX14 3FE
United Kingdom
Tel: +44 (0)1865 319700
Email: enquiries@brf.org.uk
Website: www.brf.org.uk
BRF is a Registered Charity

ISBN 978 0 85746 068 4

First published 2011
This edition 2011
10 9 8 7 6 5 4 3 2 1 0

Acknowledgments
Scripture quotations are taken from the Contemporary English Version of the Bible published by HarperCollins Publishers,
copyright © 1991, 1992, 1995 American Bible Society.

A catalogue record for this book is available from the British Library

Printed in Singapore by Craft Print International Ltd

The paper used in the production of this publication was supplied by mills that source their raw materials from sustainably
managed forests. Soy-based inks were used in its printing and the laminate film is biodegradable.

Messy Crafts

A craft-based journal

for Messy Church members

Lucy Moore

This book is dedicated with much love to my superstar goddaughter, Verity,
and her family: Kathryn, Tim and Romilly.

Acknowledgments

Thanks to the creative team at St Wilfrid's Messy Church, especially Lesley Baker, Denise Williams, Jackie Tutt, Bob and Louise Woodward, Sonia Passingham, Vicki Turner, Val Strutt, Paula Roxby and Jennifer Hall, Marlene Wylie, Colin and Angela Brown, Frank Aldous, David and Jenny Collins.
    More websites and craft books than I can list have given me inspiration for the ideas in this book.

Contents

Foreword

Craft has undergone a renaissance in recent years, which confirms my belief that craft matters. To be able to 'think with our hands' has great value. Creativity is in our DNA and fundamentally important in ensuring our well-being. Unfortunately, due to our modern way of life, these activities have been largely neglected. How exciting, then, that this book provides routes, signposts and stimuli for individuals and groups to find ways back to engaging in creative doing and thinking in our churches.

Made easy, these pages will serve to inspire and resource you effectively and powerfully in your planning. The many ideas, suggestions and starting points demand immediate use. It is about development, adaptation and reflective practice.

What excites me about this publication in particular is the format and layout, the visual prompts and references that act as a catalyst to turbocharge the possibilities around messy spaces. It is exciting and accessible. Careful attention to detail in the mention of different levels of ability makes the activities inclusive and provides opportunities for guaranteed success and satisfaction.

The *Messy Church* series of books so far have been stimulating and provided much food for thought for church life and fellowship. Being concerned with the Why? What? and How? of Messy Church provides a much-needed framework for readers. *Messy Crafts* has a particular focus on the What? What you can do is this or that; encouraging, exploration, questioning, risk-taking and, above all, courage in the process of making.

Differentiation is the key to success. The interactive nature of this book supports the notion of personalised pages and leads me to envision what these pages may well look like in different hands with different thoughts and in different creative climates.

Marlene Wylie
Art, Craft, Design and Technology Teaching and Learning Consultant, The Learning Trust Hackney

Overview of crafts and themes

TODDLER CRAFTS 12	1. Primeval swamp gloop	2. Blob painting (splat and slap)	3. Bubble printing
More ideas	Playdough recipe Get tactile… Get your hands into…	Splatting different themes	Printing with and on different ideas
Messy moment	Critical reflection	Home prayers	Bubble prayers

SATISFYING CRAFTS 21	1. Watercolour poppies	2. Quilled invitations	3. Silhouette portraits
More ideas	Watercolour gimmicks	More quilling ideas	More ideas for portraits
Messy moment	Deserts in bloom	Colour-in cross	Our name on God's hands

PRETTY CRAFTS 30	1. Prayer notebook	2. Star name family	3. Plastic pzazz
More ideas	Other prayer crafts	Eraser people ideas	Other ideas for plastic
Messy moment	Family prayer	Clock face prayers	Rainbow prayer

(REALLY) GROSS MOTOR SKILLS CRAFTS 39	1. Paintballing the cosmos	2. Pea-oneering	3. Bashing and screwing
More ideas	More big pictures (with minimum fuss)	More messy models	Very simple bashing projects
Messy moment	Graffiti wall	The wonders of God	Body parts

WORD CRAFTS 48	1. Candle holder	2. Coat hanger words	3. Honey letters
More ideas	More ideas with words and crafts	Other ways of making writing fun	Paper ways of displaying verses
Messy moment	Draw what you see…	How do you see God?	Jesus in pictures and words

FOOD CRAFTS	57	1. Paradise garden	2. Elijah's cheesy chariot	3. DIY meals
More ideas		Other sweet food ideas	More savoury food ideas	Other meal ideas
Messy moment		Cups	Prayer about food	Decorate a table of good things

GLOBAL CRAFTS	66	1. Link church (trash fash)	2. Wall displays	3. Global art
More ideas		Other link church ideas	More wall displays on global theme	Art from other countries
Messy moment		World map	Changing the world	Fruits of the Spirit

GREAT ART	75	1. Squaring up	2. God's world	3. Models from art
More ideas		More great art ideas	More art activities	Art in technology
Messy moment		Candle flames	Painting flowers	One thing you love…

QUIET MOMENTS	84	1. Draw from the inside	2. In church	3. Model a story
More ideas		Open-ended art questions	More ideas to do in church	Drawing spiritual moments, lifelines and prayers
Messy moment		God's dream for our family	Church is most like…	Linking friends to God

REALLY MESSY CRAFTS	93	1. Paint the table	2. Messy marbling	3. Water worlds
More ideas		Big messy art	More ways to marble	More painting ideas
Messy moment		The woman with perfume	Calming the storm	Zacchaeus and Jesus' invitation

Introduction

This book is more—and less—than a craft book! Think of it more as a scrapbook or journal: something to scribble in and doodle on, something to make your own, to brighten up with bright colours and stick Post-it notes in. It will be unique to your family or church by the time you're done with it: a memory book of conversations, points of view and prayers as well as all those wonderful messy things you've made. It's designed to be part of everyday life, dog-eared, splodged, loved and used, not to be kept unopened on a high shelf in pristine condition and unloved. Rather like your local church, in fact—or life, or families.

It's less than a craft book because there aren't detailed instructions for every single craft. (There really isn't a need to provide them when the internet can give them at the click of a mouse.) What's really needed is inspiration, so we've tried to cram in as many ideas as we can, so that you can then search for more details on the internet or in books, if needed.

Messy families are always on the look-out for craft ideas. This book tries to inspire some ideas instead of just churning out suggestions that you can use just once. So there's plenty of space to scribble your own thoughts on the pages: your ideas for how these crafts might fit with your themes, websites, or adaptations you could make to improve them. So get out the gel pens, glitter and glue and brighten it up as you go along.

You might like to use it to help plan sessions, to suggest ideas to your Messy Church planning team or to have fun at home with your own family.

In a Messy Church session, we need to provide crafts for all sorts of different groups of people—young, old, male, female, dextrous and frankly clumsy, active and meditative—so the idea is that the chapter headings will provide a framework to check that you're supplying a wide range of activities. You might pick one craft from each chapter or just use the chapter titles to guide your planning each month.

We've added some Bible themes that relate to specific craft ideas, but many of the ideas cover such a rich seam of biblical themes and concepts that it would be hard to mention them all under one heading.

You'll find a 'Messy moment' every few pages: an activity to do together to help you chat, think, pray or just reflect as a family or friendship group. You don't have to be a Christian to do them. Anyone can enjoy flexing their spiritual muscles with them, though they are Jesus-centred, as we believe Jesus is pretty hot on spirituality. Where there's a bit from the Bible, it's usually from a modern translation (the Contemporary English Version), or a rewording of what it says in a Bible. You might want to check out the real thing in your own Bible.

It was hard to find chapter titles that didn't exclude certain people. Yes, most toddlers enjoy playdough, but so do most teenagers. Yes, some boys enjoy hurling painty balls very hard at a wall, but so do a worrying number of grannies. So they're just broadbrush titles, not, for example, 'These crafts are ONLY for people over 65'.

Health and safety

Health and safety is, of course, important, but you will already be aware of many of the issues and hazards and know how to avoid them. For example, you'll want to consider food allergies, objects that are too small for babies to play with, heavy objects, fire and blades, but you probably already err on the side of taking sensible risks rather than living in PC / insurance claim terror. You may already feel that it's much more important, in the long term, to learn to use dangerous things responsibly, or to discover what 'consequences' are, than to avoid anything remotely risky. In families, we all know that accidents happen and that it's probably far more damaging for children to be protected from everything than to take worthwhile risks. You will know how closely your children need to be supervised and will be able to act accordingly.

And finally...

The way to end up with the most perfect crafts or pictures is for the one artistic person in your church or family to produce them and give them to you, wrapped in clear plastic. The way to end up with the most perfect thoughts about God is for the one really clever person in your church or family to tell you what to think and for you to remember that thought. But that's not what Messy Church is about. It's about exploring, questioning, and not being afraid of getting it wrong, of failing. It's about having guts, wasting and searching and giving it a go and being ourselves, not trying to be the people we think we ought to be. It's very messy, just as great artists are very messy and just as God enjoys working with people who know they're a mess. So these aren't prepackaged crafts; these are starting points for you to get creative with and improve beyond anything I could dream of.

Have fun! Get messy!

Toddler crafts

Primeval swamp gloop

Before God separated the water from the land, it must have been so messy! Mess about with this swamp gloop and talk about messy beginnings.

You will need

2 cups cornflour

1 cup water

Food colouring (optional)

Glitter (optional)

Mix everything together with your hands to make a thick sludge. Set it out in a deep tray or wide bowl and simply play with it. Try hitting its surface, modelling it, or letting it run through your fingers. Provide a few tools to use with it: a sieve, spoon or cup.

Variations on the theme of gloop

Playdough recipe

1 cup plain flour

1 cup boiling water

1 tablespoon cooking oil

2 teaspoons cream of tartar

½ cup salt

Food colouring

Stir everything up in a saucepan on a very low heat until the contents thicken into a dough. Alternatively, microwave the ingredients together on high power for 1½ minutes, stir, then microwave again for a further 1½ minutes.

Notes

Bible themes

- Being washed clean
- Finding unexpected treasure (if lucky dips are hidden in it)
- Hebrew brick builders in Egypt
- Noah's flood mud

Other themes

Simply have gloop or playdough in a corner alongside comfy chairs for anyone to enjoy as a first stage in 'Getting messy'.

Get tactile with... bark, mud, sand, water, paint, glue, soap flakes whisked into water, shaving foam...

Get your hands into... bowls of porridge, mushy peas, jelly, instant whip puddings, pasta, dried pulses or beans. (You might want to ask around for out-of-date foodstuffs rather than using edible ones, as food is primarily for eating.)

Messy moment

Date

Learning from experience

This is something important that happened to us this month:

It made us feel…

We think it made God feel…

This is what we'd like to say…

This is what we'd like to do…

Blob painting (splat and slap)

1. Take a piece of paper and fold it in half.

2. Unfold. On one half of the paper, close to the fold, paint three squares.

3. Fold again and press the halves firmly together.

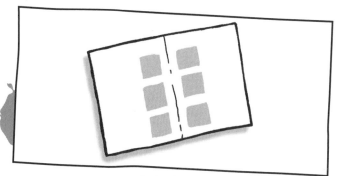

4. Unfold.

5. Now add details with a felt-tipped pen. Add the words that Jesus said: 'There are many rooms in my Father's house… I am going there to prepare a place for each of you.'

Splatting different themes

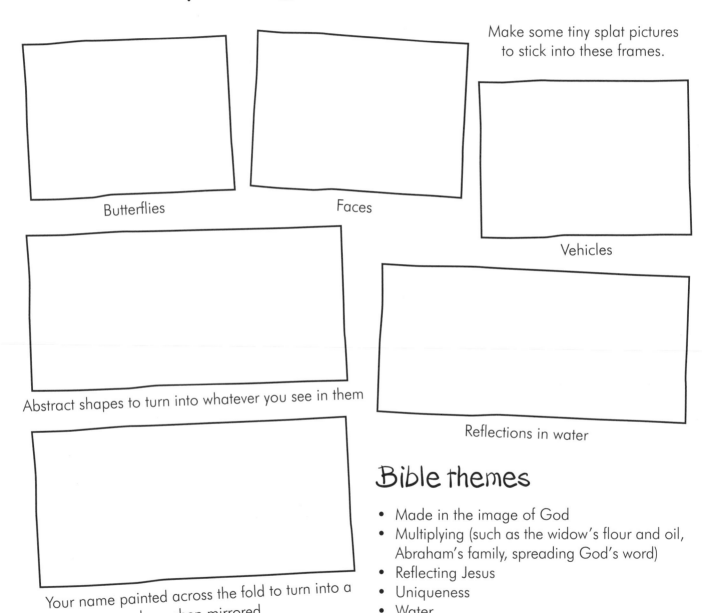

Make some tiny splat pictures to stick into these frames.

Butterflies

Faces

Vehicles

Abstract shapes to turn into whatever you see in them

Reflections in water

Your name painted across the fold to turn into a bug when mirrored

Bible themes

- Made in the image of God
- Multiplying (such as the widow's flour and oil, Abraham's family, spreading God's word)
- Reflecting Jesus
- Uniqueness
- Water

Messy moment

Home prayers

Who would you like God to bless? What about people who have no home? Draw one person in each window.

Date

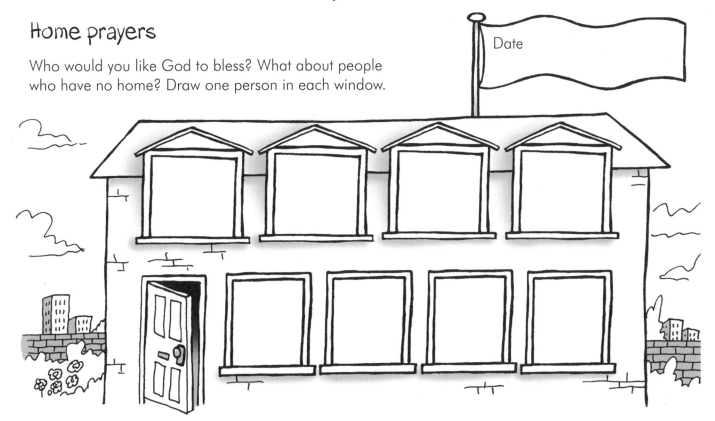

Write in the bricks…

A person I could build up is…

One thing I could do to build a better world is…

The foundations of my life are…

17

Bubble printing

1. The prodigal son might have dreamed about all the good things at home when he was far away from the farm. Draw some of the things he might have missed.

2. Now blob some paint, washing-up liquid and a little water into a small dish and stir with a straw.

3. Blow into the mixture so that it bubbles up.

4. Lower your drawing, face down, on to the bubbles and lift it off.

5. Repeat with other colours until you have made the background as dreamy as you want.

Bible themes

- Dreams of Joseph, the wise men, and Pharaoh
- People in pain, like the people Jesus healed
- Prophetic visions of Ezekiel, Isaiah, John, and Daniel
- The Lord's Prayer

Other themes

- Dreams of a better world

Printing with and on different ideas

Print with

Kitchen tools

String

Bubblewrap

Nuts and bolts

Hands, fingertips, feet

Fruit punnet netting

Fruit and vegetables

Sponge

Fish (see Japanese art of Gyotaku)

Print on

Dark paper, light paper

Tea towels

Dishcloths

Sheets

Tablecloths

T-shirts, baseball caps

Big leaves

Plates, tiles, mugs

Flowerpots

Paving slabs

Shaped card

Messy moment

Bubble prayers

Date

Big prayers

and

small prayers

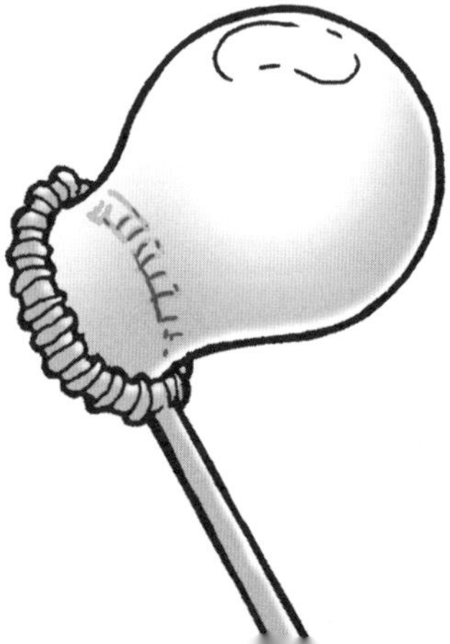

A prayer we're just starting to pray.

 # Watercolour poppies

Consider the poppies…

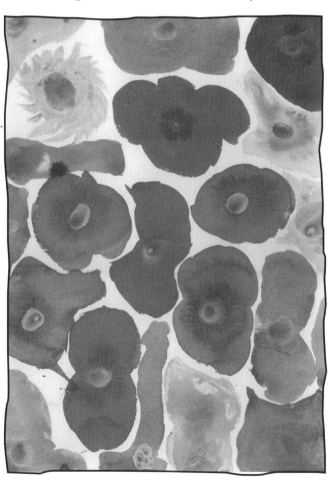

Instructions

Have a limited range of watercolours available. In the centre of the paper write a title, if desired: Jesus said, 'Look how the wild flowers grow…' With a brush, paint a solid circle of one colour on watercolour paper. It doesn't matter if it's not an even circle.

Dip your thumb in a contrasting colour and make a thumbprint on top of the first circle. It makes an abstract poppy shape. Add more poppies in different colours and sizes to cover the paper.

Bible themes

- Creation
- Flowers blooming in the desert (Isaiah 35:1–2)
- Easter (you could paint eggs rather than flowers)
- Weddings

Other themes

- Colour
- Ecology
- Mothering Sunday
- Spring and summer

Watercolour gimmicks: More instant ideas with paint and paper

Scrunch up clingfilm, dip in paint and press on to paper. Allow to dry before you peel it off. The prints will look like rocks.

Outline a shape on the paper using a brush dipped in water, then paint colour into the shape. The edges will be sharper.

Draw a picture in white candlewax and paint over it.

Drop a little table salt on the damp paint and let it dry mottled.

Think extreme crafts: hire a badge machine, an enamelling kiln, soap-making kit or felting kit. Many kits are available from Infinite Crafts: www.inf.co.uk

Messy moment

Deserts in bloom

Date

Thirsty deserts will be glad;
barren lands will celebrate and blossom with flowers.
(Isaiah 35:1)

Here are some areas that we think are dry and dusty like a desert.

We would like Jesus' living water to change them…

Here are some blooming, wonderful things we thank God for…

23

2 Quilled invitations

You are invited to Messy Church

on:

at:

We do things like this

You will need:

A quilling tool

Quilling strips (best to buy ready-made ones before you see if you can cut your own)

Scissors

Glue

Cocktail stick

Card

1. Take a quilling strip and thread it into the tool so that as little end as possible shows. Twirl it between the fingers of the hand that's not holding the tool so that it makes a tightish spiral around the tool.

2. Free the twirl from the tool by turning the tool back the opposite way for just a quarter of a turn and sliding the twirl off.

3. Let the twirl spring out as much as you want it to, and then secure the end of the strip, using a dot of glue on a cocktail stick and holding it for a few seconds to dry. Glue the twirl to the invitation card.

More quilling ideas

Tight twirls

Eye-shaped twirls

Loose twirls

Squished twirls

Letter twirls

Hide a Bible verse inside a twirl in tiny writing

Use the twirls to decorate:

Badges

Crosses

Boxes

Fridge magnets

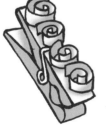

Pencil tops

Bookmarks

Gift tags

Clothes pegs

Collages

Photo frames

Greetings cards

Messy moment

Date

Colour-in cross

Colour in one letter on the cross for each broken, hurting or ill person or place you know.

Colour in a background section of the cross for every beautiful, joyful and blessed person or place you know.

3 Silhouette portraits

Shine a really bright light on to a wall. Sit sideways on between the light and the wall.

Let your friend or family member place a sheet of dark paper on the wall and draw round the shadow of your face profile very carefully with a soft pencil, including every stray wisp of hair, so that you can cut it out and mount it on an oval background of a contrasting colour. Older people might like to cut it out with a craft knife.

(You can also make silhouettes with digital photos, using computer programmes such as Photoshop.)

Bible themes

- God's love for each person
- Made in the image of God
- Every hair on your head is counted (Psalm 139)
- 'I have called you by name' (Isaiah 43:1)
- Beauty (Esther)
- Parts of the body (1 Corinthians 12:12–27)

More ideas for portraits

Microscopes

Put one of your hairs under a microscope and have a look at it. Draw what you see.

Instant supermodel

- Cut out a body from a magazine.
- Cut out a photo of your head.
- Glue one to the other.

Printing

Make your portrait in thumbprints or with string printing.

Peculiar portraits

Have a range of geometric shapes, in card or funky foam or felt, to glue together to make your family portrait.

Notes

Messy moment

Date _____

Our name on God's hands

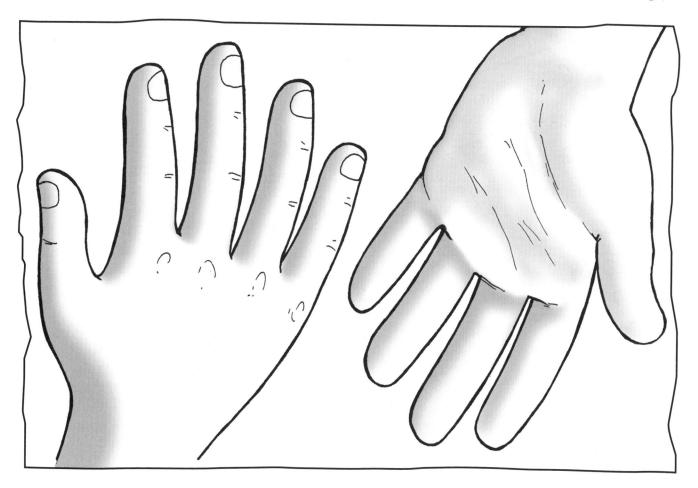

'A picture of your home is drawn on my hand. I'm always thinking about you!' (see Isaiah 49:16)

Who might be drawn on the back of God's hand to remind him of them?
Who might be drawn on his palm, as if to keep them safe?

Pretty crafts

1 Prayer notebook

Turn an ordinary, plain-cover notebook into a special notebook and write your prayers inside in secret.

Take a small square of felt and glue it on to a slightly larger square of felt in a contrasting colour. Thread a needle and sew one or more beads or sequins on to the squares. Sewing through the double thickness of felt will help to hold them firmly together. Glue the decoration to the front of the notebook.

Other prayer crafts

Prayer pot

Write the names of people you want to pray for on squares of card. Pull one out of the pot each day.

Prayer tree

Clip on to your tree the names of people you want to pray for.

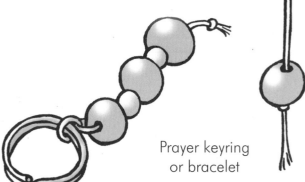

Prayer keyring or bracelet

Use one bead for each person or place you want to pray for.

Prayer candle holder

Light the candle when you pray.

Messy moment

Date

Family prayer

Christians all round the world and all through the ages have prayed Jesus' prayer. What patterns, pictures or words does each phrase make you think of?

Our Father in heaven	Hallowed be your name	Your will be done
Give us today our daily bread	Forgive us our sins	Lead us not into temptation
Deliver us from evil	For the kingdom	Amen

2 Star name family

God thinks your family is a star family!

Write your name in big letters and trail glue over the writing. Stick foil stars on the lines of glue so that your name is written in the stars!

Eraser people ideas

Use slices of potato or a bendy eraser to print people on…

- wrapping paper
- cardboard files
- picture frames
- writing paper

Use for pictures of crowds, such as Jesus feeding 5000 people, the Israelites crossing the Red Sea or themes of…

- family
- school
- friends
- self
- buildings
- trees
- animals
- flowers

Messy moment

Date

Clock face prayers

What can you praise God for at different times of the day and night?

'I will always praise the Lord.' (Psalm 34:1)

3 Plastic pzazz

- Open out a laminating pouch.

- Drop flattish sequins and beads and scraps of coloured foil or card into groups: red shapes to represent Jesus on the cross on Good Friday; dark shapes to represent his time in the tomb; and yellow and gold for Easter Day. (You could have a piece of paper with squares marked out, placed behind your plastic as guidelines.)

- Close and laminate.

- Cut each group out in a square shape.

- Punch holes in each square with a hole punch and thread together with shiny thread.

- Hang the story sequence where it catches the light and be ready to tell anyone the story behind it.

ANGELS!

LIGHT!

TREASURE!

Other ideas for plastic

Use the same technique to…

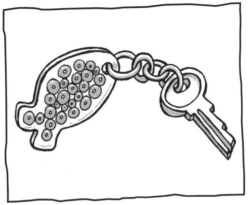

cut out in the shape of a cross or fish for a
necklace, key fob or phone charm.

decorate and laminate a short prayer
such as the Jesus Prayer: 'Lord Jesus
Christ, have mercy on me, a sinner.'

RICHES!

INHERITANCE!

STARS!

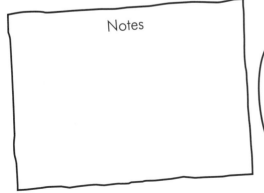

Notes

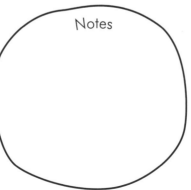

Notes

make a notebook cover.

Messy moment

Rainbow prayer

Date

Colour the rainbow and pray for the people as you colour.

People in countries at war
People in prison and their families
People without enough money
People who are ill
People at my work, school or college
My family
Me

'Each morning you listen to my prayer, as I bring my requests to you and wait for your reply.'
(Psalm 5:3)

(Really) gross motor skills crafts

1 Paintballing the cosmos

This is possibly a craft for outside, unless small non-bouncy balls and much protection are used. (Hours of fun for all who have to clean up!)

Have a variety of balls, white and yellow powder paint and poster paint, and a HUGE sheet of dark paper or card against a wall.

Write the title on the sheet of paper in gold or silver pen: 'God also made the stars.' Have a go at making your own cosmos.

Dip a ball in the paint and throw it at the paper. Repeat with gentler or harder throws and with different sorts of balls:

beanbag

foam ball

rubber ball

beach ball

Bible themes

- Impact of our actions on others
- Expressing anger
- Hitting or failing to hit the target (Romans 3:21)
- David and Goliath
- Hailstones and fireballs
- Light (such as fireworks)

tennis ball

pingpong ball

football

juggling ball

More big pictures (with minimum fuss)

Add your own ideas next to the paper splodges.

 Ride a bike, trike or scooter through paint.

 Garden spray bottles of paint make good dribbly effects.

 Dip a toy car or tractor in paint and wheel it over paper.

 Print with large car-washing sponges dipped in paint or ketchup.

 Dribble a pattern of glue and shake sand or glitter over it.

 Dip marbles or balls in paint and roll them over paper on a tray.

Messy moment

Graffiti wall

The writing's on the wall. Look up the story in Daniel 5.

What do you think Jesus would like to transform in your life? Graffiti it on this wall.

Drawn by:

Date:

Pea-oneering

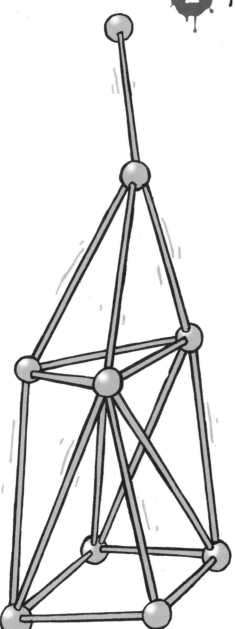

Soak dried peas for about five hours or until firm but soft. Drain them and use them with cocktail sticks to make the tower of Babel.

More themes

- Constellations
- Other buildings: the highest point of the temple, biblical house
- Animals
- Abstract shape: 'My family is like…' 'I feel like….' 'My life looks like…'
- Molecular structures

Notes

More messy models

Junk modelling: provide clean junk (especially giant cardboard boxes), string, scissors and sticky tape

Duct tape modelling

Aluminium foil

Newspaper rolls

Rectangular or finger biscuits, and icing or chocolate spread, to build into a 3D model

Styrofoam or polystyrene

Paper or plastic straws

Elastic bands stretched over frameworks (such as coat hangers or sturdy boxes)

Packaging noodles made of cornstarch, dampened and stuck together

Check out Inuksuk on the web: Inuit stone balancing

Messy moment

The wonders of God

'The heavens keep telling the wonders of God!' (Psalm 19:1)

What might the heavens be saying, if they could speak your language, from their perspectives of life, the universe and everything?

Date

3 Bashing and screwing

Hammered cross

- You need two smallish rectangles of wood, hammers, nails and wood glue.
- Nail or glue the wood together in the centre.
- Add nails where you want.
- You could wind shiny thread around them to represent resurrection power.

Notes

Notes

Very simple bashing projects

Screw a hook into a wooden shape for a coat hook. Decorate with paint.

Nail a cube on to a flat boat shape for Noah's ark, Peter's fishing boat or Jonah's ship.

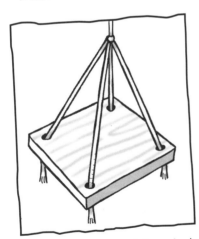

Make a bird table. Drill four holes in a square of wood. Thread cord through the holes, make a knot underneath the base and knot together above the base, then hang from a tree.

Hammer a drawing pin through a foil pie dish into a soft base, such as a polystyrene tray.

Other gross and fine motor skills might involve:

- Embossing
- Origami
- Den building
- Lighting candles (under supervision with matches)
- Carving soap

46

Messy moment

Body parts

'Together you are the body of Christ.' (1 Corinthians 12:27)

Who is like which part of the body?

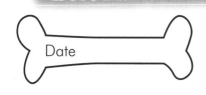

Date

Who else needs prayer?

Write or draw them in the bones.

47

1 Candle holder

Jesus is the light of the world.

On a clean glass jar or glass, use a glass-writing pen to write and decorate the verse. You could also use acrylic paint or nail varnish, though it gets very pongy. Make sure the decoration is on the OUTSIDE of the glass.

It's best not to wash up the glass or the decoration falls off, however long-lasting the glass paints promise to be.

Choose or adapt a short verse (such as John 8:12) or just use one significant word.

More ideas with words and crafts

- Powder chalk all over shiny card, then write in it with a finger.
- Scratch words on multicoloured card that's been painted over with black paint and allowed to dry.

- Make, write and illustrate your own Bible story book.
- Write a message in chalk outside in HUGE letters that can only be read from a high place.

- Write on T-shirts or caps (and see different printing ideas on page 19).
- Make a mosaic message on a tile or plaque.
- Turn a verse into txt.
- Storyboard a story.

Messy moment

Date

Draw what you see...

What do you read when you're unhappy?
Read out what David read when he was miserable.

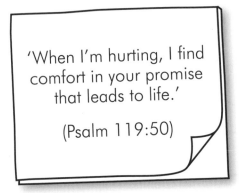

'When I'm hurting, I find
comfort in your promise
that leads to life.'

(Psalm 119:50)

Now everyone gets a sticky note and draws a
picture that stands for something they know God
has promised them. Stick all the notes on this
page around David's words.
Each person might like to say a prayer that
goes with their drawing.

2 Coat hanger words

- Cut out letters from magazines and newspapers.
- Select letters that spell your message.
- Glue each one to a separate small square of thick card. (You could use bottle tops, unwanted Scrabble tiles or mosaic tiles instead.)
- Tape a piece of craft wire to the back of each square.
- Wind the craft wire round the coat hanger base in the right order and with the letters all facing the same way.

'God loved the people of this world so much that he gave his only Son,
so that everyone who has faith in him will have eternal life and never really die.'
(John 3:16)

Other ways of making writing fun

'Ransom note': cut out letters from newspapers to form the message

'Autograph book' of everybody's favourite Bible verses

Lucky dip prize (a message plus a wrapped sweet)

Bury verses in the sand for a treasure hunt

Mini scrolls: make with parchment paper on cocktail sticks, decorated with a bead stuck on to each spike

Quill

Prick out words with a pin

Write in invisible ink

Chalk

Mud or clay

Charcoal

Letters punched out in holes

Pokerwork on wood

Calligraphy pens

Write with food colouring or icing on toast or biscuits

Letters squidged out from playdough

Messy moment

Date _____

How do you see God?

God is like a _____

He's as _____ as a _____

He's _____ like _____

He's _____ er than a _____

And he's the _____ est and _____ est and _____ est!

③ Honey letters

The psalmist wrote, 'Your words taste so sweet to me! Sweeter than a honey hit on my taste buds!' (see Psalm 119:103).

A traditional Jewish way of teaching children the alphabet was to make the shape of the letters in honey for the children to trace with their fingers and savour.

Drip a simple word on to a piece of bread or a clean plate using one of the following: honey, pouring syrup, ketchup, chocolate sauce, cheese spread from a tube, salad cream (ugh), sweet chilli sauce, glacé icing sprinkled with hundreds-and-thousands, slightly melted ice cream, Marmite, jam... or a mixture of all of them (double ugh).
Trace with a finger and lick the finger!

Paper ways of displaying verses

Non-edible version...

Drip PVA glue in the shape of the word or verse, and sprinkle with glitter,
foil confetti, stars or scraps cut from coloured paper. You could also use out-of-date
rice and pulses, or flower heads, pips, seeds, sand, wax crayon shavings,
funky foam chips, felt scraps, beads…

Use to make a…

Label

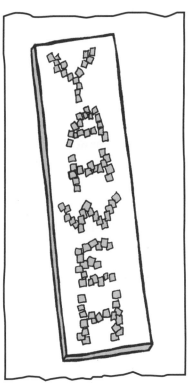

Bookmark

Door hanger

Messy moment

Date _____

Jesus in pictures and words

Fill in the letters with drawings, doodles, words and Bible verses that celebrate who Jesus is.

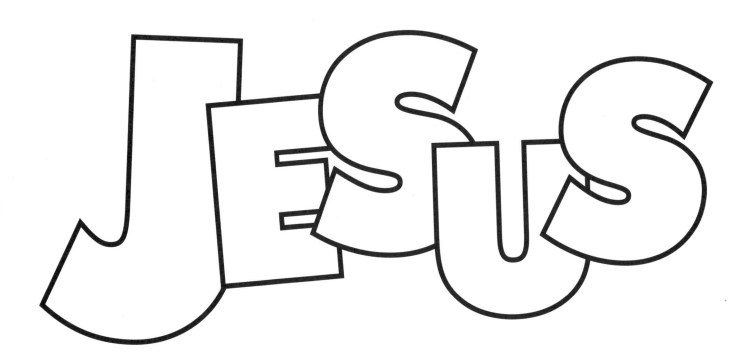

1 Paradise garden

Create an edible landscape

Queen Esther's royal playground

Garden of Eden

Heaven

King David's palace garden

Use any of the following:

- fruit segments
- biscuits
- sweets
- strawberry laces
- readymade icing
- writing icing or glacé icing
- chocolate sticks
- mini marshmallows
- jelly babies
- buns
- cake pieces
- chocolate coins
- chocolate leaves
- lollipop 'trees'

A small chocolate fountain might be playing in the centre.

If it's a large group activity, each person could make their section of the garden on a foil tray. The trays can then be fitted together but eaten later by the person who made the section.

Other sweet food ideas

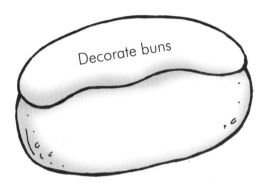

Decorate buns

Dried fruit dip

Shakes

Decorate
biscuits

Smoothies

Bake biscuits

Gingerbread

Fruit kebab
dip

Tiffin

Scones

Peppermint
creams

Hoops breakfast
cereal bracelet

Mixed juice
cocktails

Messy moment

Date _____

Cups

King David: 'You fill my cup until it overflows.' (Psalm 23:5)

What's in your cup?

Peace joy
love
contentment
long life friends
family health
hope future
purpose

Blessings and hardships

Pain cross
hurting
betrayal loneliness
no friends
no home death

Jesus: 'Father, I wish you would take this cup away. But if you want me to drink it, I will.'
(Mark 14:36)

2 Elijah's cheesy chariot

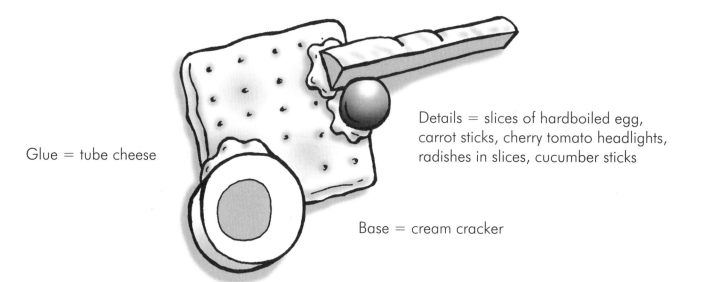

Glue = tube cheese

Details = slices of hardboiled egg, carrot sticks, cherry tomato headlights, radishes in slices, cucumber sticks

Base = cream cracker

A blob of chilli sauce on the wheels makes it a chariot of fire.

Elijah and Elisha were walking along… when suddenly there appeared between them a flaming chariot pulled by fiery horses. (2 Kings 2:11)

Don't forget Joseph's chariot in Genesis 46:29; Pharaoh's chariots in Exodus 14:6–28; Solomon's chariots in 1 Kings 10:26; Philip and the Ethiopian official in Acts 8:26–38 and oodles more, plus any story involving travel.

More savoury food ideas

Paint food colouring on bread

cream cheese

Marmite

plain yoghurt

Savoury dips

salsa

ketchup

Cheese straws

Make up cheese straw mixture from a recipe. Roll out and cut into different shapes with a pastry cutter.

Garnishes to make plates attractive: tomato flowers, radish roses, carrot cogs, cucumber tassels, cucumber balls (like melon balls), courgette strip fans

Construction with food might contain:

- Cheese strings
- Cheese squares / triangles / circles
- Crisps
- Cheese biscuits
- Twiglets
- Hula hoops
- Teddy crisps
- Salad vegetables
- Raw peas
- Salami slices
- Cooked sausage circles
- Edible leaves (herbs, nasturtiums, lettuce)

Messy moment

Date _____

Prayer about food

1 Kings 17:1–7 (the ravens bringing food to Elijah)

Where's Elijah?

Don't talk with your beak full.

Jesus said:

Don't worry about having something to eat.

(Luke 12:22)

What we could do to help people with very little food:

- _____
- _____
- _____
- _____

Thank you, God, for all the food you give us, especially...

Unsuspecting quail (see Exodus 16:13)

3 DIY meals

Hotdog in a blanket

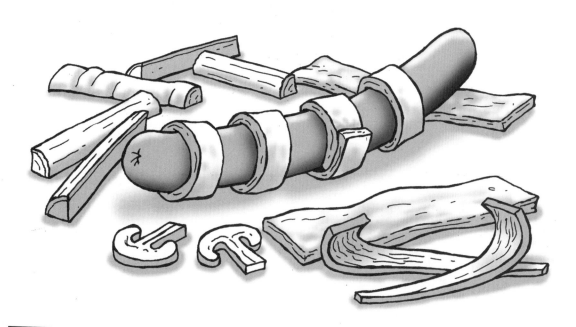

You will need:

- Tinned hotdog sausage or similar veggie version.
- Puff pastry, rolled out thin, cut into strips and wrapped round sausage.
- Vegetables tucked in if desired: sliced mushroom, carrot, courgette, pepper...

1. Place on greaseproof paper.

2. Glaze with beaten egg if desired.

3. Cook in a hot oven until golden brown (about 10–20 minutes).

Other meal ideas

- Pizza: decorate a pizza base or slice of baguette cut in half lengthways with pizza sauce / tomato puree, usual pizza toppings and cheese.

- Tortilla wrap: Fill your own wrap with cooked chicken, veggie shapes, salsa, lettuce, cucumber, tomato, avocado, sour cream.

- Skewer: fill your own with vegetables and meat and cook in hot oven or on a barbecue.

- Secret pie: put a filling (cheese, mushroom, tuna, baked bean, cooked mince, veggie mince) between two puff pastry circles, seal with beaten egg, glaze and cook.

Messy moment

Date

Decorate a table of good things

Wow! Thanks!

Many people will come from everywhere...

... to enjoy the feast in the kingdom of heaven.

(Matthew 8:11)

You treat me to a feast, while my enemies watch.

(Psalm 23:5)

What good things has God put on your table? Can you draw them?

65

Global crafts

Link church (trash fash)

Dressing up

Do some research into the styles people wear in your link church overseas.

Can you make…

hats?

clothes?

shoes?

accessories?

like theirs from…

sheets

bin bags

newspaper

wrapping paper

sticky tape

staplers

string

Why do you think people wear clothes like this?

Is it about fashion, comfort, culture, climate, work?

What's the same as the clothes you wear? What's different?

Other link church ideas

Craft inspiration

Check out your link church's country.

Is there anything you could play with, recreate, learn from, develop, copy or borrow a pattern from?

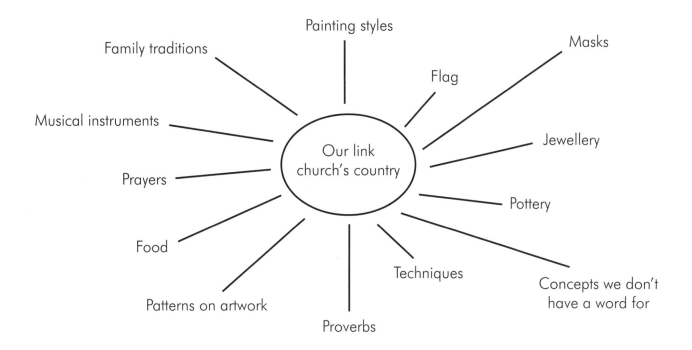

'I saw a large crowd… from every country, and they stood before the throne of Jesus.'
(Revelation 7:9)

Messy moment

Date _____

World map

 People we know   People in need   **M** Other Messy Churches round the world
(check the directory on www.messychurch.org.uk)

Let's pray! Mark on the map who you're praying for.

2 Wall displays

Fairtrade

Chocolate

Bananas

Beauty

Cotton clothes

Sugar

Cocoa

'See that justice is done, let mercy be your first concern, and humbly obey your God.' (Micah 6:8)

More wall displays on global theme

reduce

reuse

recycle

rejoice

small green steps

Our town

I'm lovin' it!

I'm livin' it!

A Rocha

Christian Aid

Fair Trade

the people

the places

the future

Recycling

Local environment

Enjoying nature

Make poverty history

Rogation Sunday

Messy moment

Date _____

Changing the world

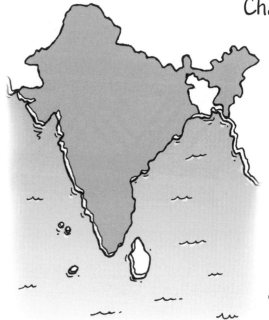

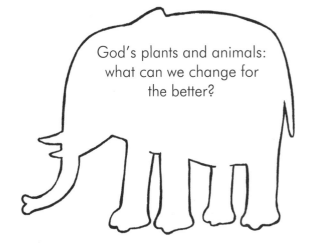

God's people:
what can we
change for
the better?

God's lands
and seas:
what can we
change for the
better?

God's plants and animals:
what can we change for
the better?

God, help us to care for your world.

3 Global art

Stringy symbols

- Copy some Adinkra symbols from the internet or from Divine chocolate wrappers.
- Trace one on to card.
- Dribble glue over the pattern's lines.
- Stick string on to the glue and allow to dry.
- Roller or sponge it with paint.
- Print it.
- Frame it.

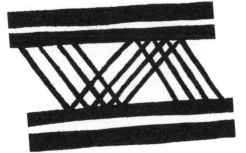

Owoforo adobe = standing firm

Nyame nti = faith in God

Kete pa = good marriage

Mpatapo = peacemaking

Art from other countries

Take a picture from another country and use its ideas to make your own art...

Cut out your favourite small detail from the picture and include it in a design of your own

Find a pattern in the picture and use it upside down, back to front and broken up to make another pattern

Copy a carving in soft soap

Add speech bubbles to any characters in the picture

Notes

Notes

Notes

Cut out hexagons from photos of the country and glue them together in a patchwork

Use the same colours to paint a different scene

Messy moment

Date _____

Fruits of the Spirit

If you live by the Spirit, you're full of...

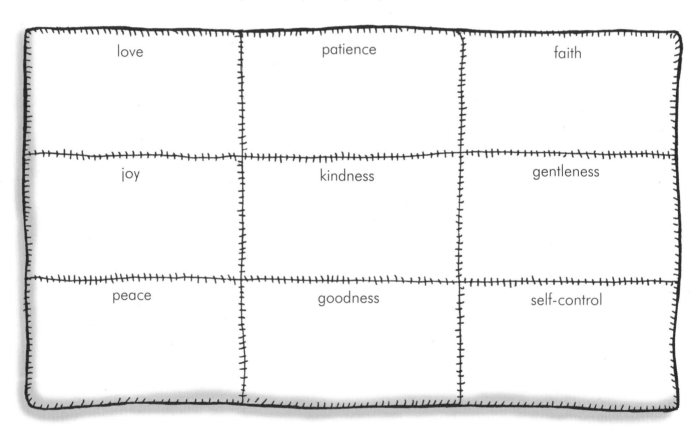

love	patience	faith
joy	kindness	gentleness
peace	goodness	self-control

(See Galatians 5:22–23)

What symbol or pattern or colour would you draw in for each of these wonderful things?

Great art

 Squaring up

1. Make two large copies of a picture.
2. Rule one off into twelve squares or rectangles and cut them out.
3. Give a square to each person or family to copy on to a larger piece of paper of the same shape.
4. Reassemble the bigger pictures to make a new, bigger, messier masterpiece.
5. Display it with the complete copy.

More great art ideas

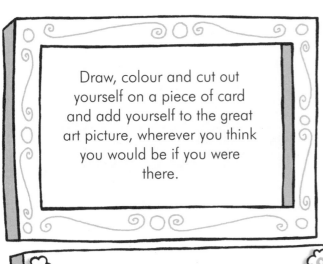

Draw, colour and cut out yourself on a piece of card and add yourself to the great art picture, wherever you think you would be if you were there.

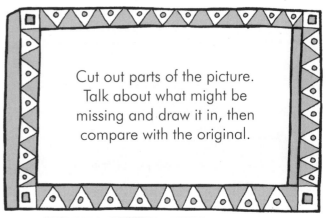

Cut out parts of the picture. Talk about what might be missing and draw it in, then compare with the original.

Draw the next moment in the story.

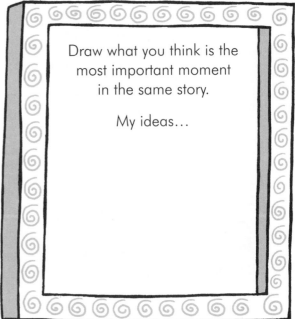

Draw what you think is the most important moment in the same story.

My ideas...

Messy moment

Date _____

Candle flames

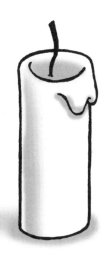

Draw and colour a candle flame for each person you pray for today.

2 God's world

How do artists wonder at God's world?

Look at their pictures of natural things.

What are they trying to say about this flower, tree or scene? For example…

Picasso's dove

Van Gogh's sunflowers

Rousseau's jungles

Klimt's trees

Rejoice in God's world by drawing something in your garden or park in the same style or colour.

More art activities

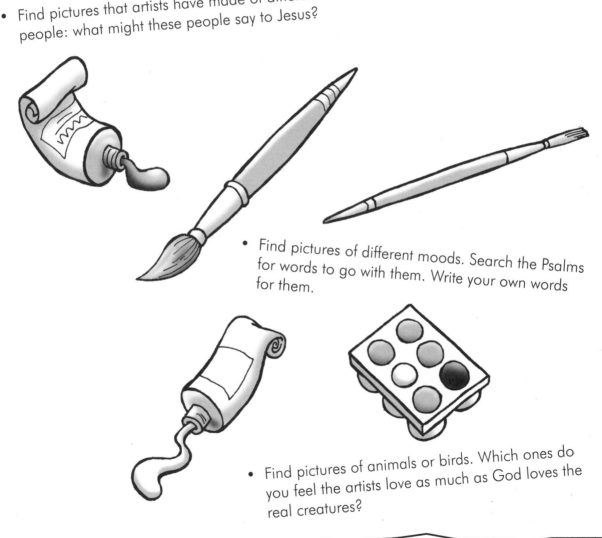

- Find pictures that artists have made of different people: what might these people say to Jesus?

- Find pictures of different moods. Search the Psalms for words to go with them. Write your own words for them.

- Find pictures of animals or birds. Which ones do you feel the artists love as much as God loves the real creatures?

Messy moment

Painting flowers

Date

Find a flower
or twig or leaf.
Really look at it.
Now really, really
look at it!

Paint your own
picture of it in
the frame. What
does your painting
say about your
feelings?

What does it tell
you about who
made it?

3 Models from art

Model it! (Act it!)

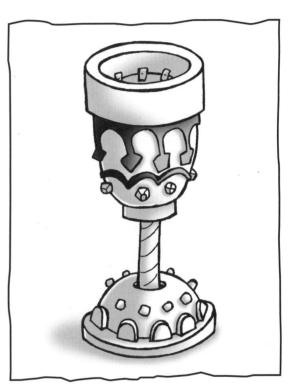

Make a model of it using a plastic goblet, foil, sticky jewels, card, paper or clay.

Find a picture of the Last Supper.

Now use real people to pose just like the people in the original picture, with the cup, and take a photo of the scene.

Look carefully at the cup Jesus uses.

Art in technology

Get digital: make a news broadcast for your story and record it with a video camera.

Record an audio commentary to go with a picture or set of photos or silent film.

Make a photo story.

Other thoughts…

Other thoughts…

Make a TV advert or radio jingle.

Make a PowerPoint of photos to go with a worship song.

Messy moment

One thing you love...

Give everyone in your family or group a sticky note. Everyone writes their name at the top. Pass the notes round the circle. Each person writes one thing they love about the person whose name is on the paper. Stick all the notes on this page.

Date: _____   By: _____

Draw from the inside

Non-dominant hand drawing

1. Listen to a worship song.

2. Draw how you feel as the song plays.

3. Listen to it again, but this time hold a crayon or chalk in your non-dominant hand.

4. Talk about what you've drawn.

God says: 'I will make you strong if you quietly trust me.' (Isaiah 30:15)

Open-ended art questions

Draw or paint...

What's God like?

What would a symbol for
you look like?

The most important people in your life

Other ideas...

- The best church
- Heaven and hell
- What is ugly?
- Your favourite moment from a story
- Your happiest memory
- Your saddest memory
  (would you draw Jesus in, too?)

Messy moment

God's dream for our family

Date

God's dream for our family might look like this…

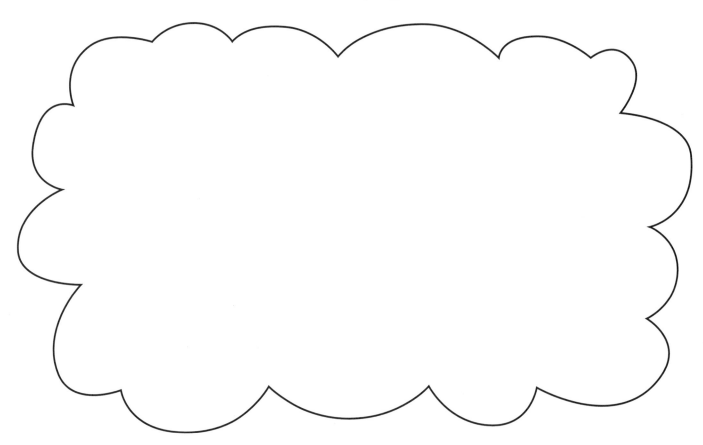

King David prayed, 'Lord God, my family and I don't deserve what you have
already done for us, and yet you have promised to do even more…
You are treating me as if I am a VIP.' (1 Chronicles 17:16–17)

2 In church

Spend five minutes looking round your church building.

What detail do you like best?

Draw it inside a heart shape
and colour it in.

More ideas to do in church

- Colour one of your stained-glass windows on acetate.
- Make a gargoyle or angel out of playdough, soap or clay.

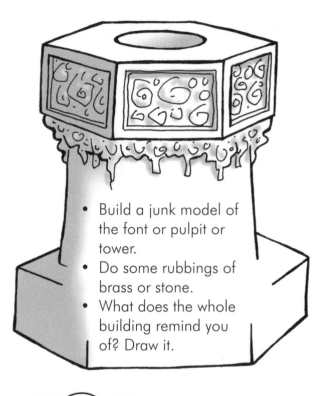

- Build a junk model of the font or pulpit or tower.
- Do some rubbings of brass or stone.
- What does the whole building remind you of? Draw it.

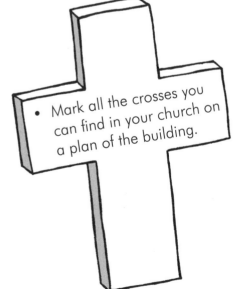

- Mark all the crosses you can find in your church on a plan of the building.

- How does the building make you feel? Can you draw the feeling?
- Take a box of crayons or paints and shade in abstract shapes on paper with all the colours you see in the church.

Messy moment

Date _____

Church is most like...

We think church is most like…

A beautiful bride for Jesus (Mark 2:18–20)

A body with different parts
(1 Corinthians 12:27)

A vine or vineyard (John 15:1–8)

A kingdom (Romans 14:17)

A building with Jesus as the cornerstone
(1 Peter 2:5–6)

A flock of sheep with a shepherd
(John 10:11)

A family with the same father
(Galatians 3:26; 4:6–7)

Something else…

89

3 Model a story

Stand in a story

- Read a Bible story.

- Make a setting for the story out of card (like a film set).

- Make figures for each person out of foil.

- Set the figures in the setting.

- Ask yourself: 'Where's Jesus in this scene? Where are we?'

- Move the figures round and see what changes in the story.

Drawing spiritual moments, lifelines and prayers

Draw your family lifeline with highs and lows.

- High points
- Low points
- Where is God at each point, do you think?

Draw yourself as a tree.

What are your roots?

What are your branches?

What is your fruit?

Draw a pattern for today.

Did you feel close to or far away from God?

Messy moment

Date _____

Linking friends to God

Praying for friends
- Write the word GOD in the square at the centre.
- Draw one of your friends in each of the smaller boxes.
- Doodle patterns for what they need prayer for.
- Add shapes linking them to God. Colour them in as you pray.

(This is how I pray for the Messy Churches on the Directory.)

Really messy crafts

1 Paint the table

Just simply paint the table...

Really messy projects link to all sorts of themes, but are also quite simple FUN.

Big messy art

Drop handfuls of powder paint over stencils or templates.

Fill waterbombs or eggshells with runny paint and drop from a great height.

On humungous sheets of paper...

Suspend bottles of glue on string and swing them over the paper to make patterns, then drop chopped-up pieces of foil over it.

Paint with wallpaper brushes and paint rollers.

Messy moment

The woman with perfume

Date _____

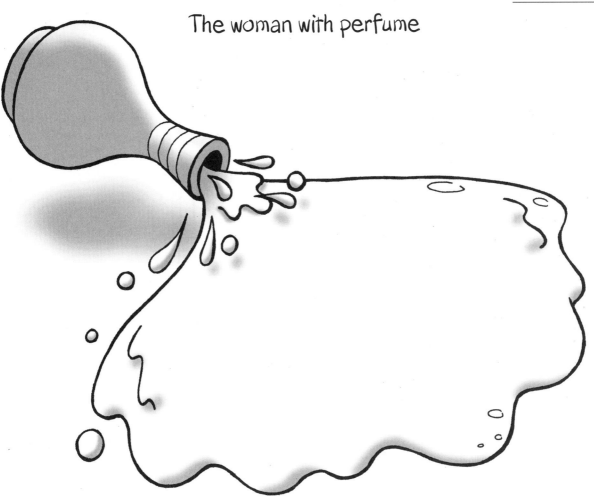

'Mary took a very expensive bottle of perfume and poured it on Jesus' feet.'
(John 12:3)

Draw or write in the perfume what you would like to pour out for him.

2 Messy marbling

1. Squirt shaving foam on to a tabletop.
2. Drip paint or food colouring on to it.
3. Swirl the colour into a marbled effect with a squidgy window cleaner.
4. Print by lowering paper on to it.
5. Scrape the remaining foam into bin bags.

More ways to marble

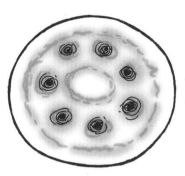

Marbling inks dripped on to the surface of water and swirled together. Drop cardboard shapes on to the surface and shake off excess water as you lift it off.

Coffee filter coloured with marker pens, then sprayed with water to make the colours spread.

Water pistols fired at paint splodges.

Acrylic inks dripped on to watercolour paper and sprayed with water: when dry, they make lovely backgrounds for collage or silhouettes.

Very classy.

Very messy.

Messy moment

Date _____

Calming the storm

Look at the story about a storm in Mark 4:35–41. If you were there, what would you be doing?
Draw yourself in the picture.

3 Water worlds

In an under-bed storage tray or baby bath with water in, build up mud islands and decorate them with sand, twigs, flowers, moss, Lego® buildings, Playmobil® people, windmills, boats, ducks…

More painting ideas

Try painting with your brush in your mouth… your toes… between your knees… behind your back…

Jumbo chalks, charcoal, or water to decorate a fence or paving stones…

Notes

Notes

Face painting… hand painting… henna designs for older people… transfer tattoos for people in a rush…

Messy moment

Date _____

Zacchaeus and Jesus' invitation

Zacchaeus met Jesus and found he wanted to change to have the best life possible (Luke 19:1–10).

Draw in your family and write what you might say if you met Jesus at this table too.

'I'm going to stop stealing and pay people back! What are you going to do?'

Index

Main crafts

Other ideas

Bible themes

Messy moments

Planning grid for Messy Church

Theme: _____   Date: _____

Crafts	Preparation	Craft Leader	Notes

Notes

Notes

Notes

Notes

Notes

Notes

Notes

Notes

Notes

Notes

Notes

Notes

Notes

Notes

Messy Cooks

A handbook for Messy Church catering teams

Jane Butcher

This book is a handbook for everyone involved in Messy Church catering teams! As well as being a useful treasure store of practical and easy-to-prepare recipes for all your Messy Church events, it also provides tips on quantities, basic cooking skills, essential equipment and ideas for relating food to a Bible story, theme or festival.

There are 36 recipes in total—two delicious main courses and a scrummy dessert for every month of the year. Each recipe includes at least one helpful hint, suggested variations to ring the changes or provide a vegetarian option, and space for you to jot down your own personal reflections, comments and notes.

All the recipes have been used in real Messy Churches, tried and tested in real Messy Church kitchens by real Messy cooks, and enjoyed by real Messy Church families. One Messy cook summed it up by saying, 'We love seeing the children's faces when they come in and ask us "What's for dinner?"'

ISBN 978 0 85746 069 1   £5.99

Available from your local Christian bookshop or direct from BRF: visit www.brfonline.org.uk.

Other Messy Church® resources

Messy Church

Fresh ideas for building a Christ-centred community

Lucy Moore

Messy Church is bursting with easy-to-do ideas to draw people of all ages together and help them to experience what it means to be part of a Christian community outside of Sunday worship.

At its heart, Messy Church aims to create the opportunity for parents, carers and children to enjoy expressing their creativity, sit down together to eat a meal, experience worship and have fun within a church context.

The book sets out the theory and practice of Messy Church and offers 15 themed programme ideas to get you started, each including:

- Bible references and background information
- Suggestions for 10 easy-to-do creative art and craft activities
- Easy-to-prepare everyday recipes
- Family-friendly worship outlines

Check out the Messy Church website at www.messychurch.org.uk.

ISBN 978 1 84101 503 3   £8.99
Available from your local Christian bookshop or direct from BRF: visit www.brfonline.org.uk.

Messy Church 2

Ideas for discipling a Christ-centred community

Lucy Moore

Messy Church is growing! Since it began in 2004, many churches have picked up the idea of drawing people of all ages together and inviting them to experience fun-filled Christian community outside Sunday worship.

Following the popular Messy Church formula, *Messy Church 2* not only provides a further 15 exciting themed sessions, but also explores ways to help adults and children alike to go further and deeper with God—in other words, to grow as disciples.

As before, the material is overflowing with ideas for creativity, fun, food, fellowship and family-friendly worship, but new to *Messy Church 2* are 'take-away' ideas to help people think about their Messy Church experience between the monthly events.

Across the year, the 15 themes explore:

- Loving God, our neighbours and our world
- The life of Jesus: growing up
- Bible women: Ruth, Hannah and Esther
- Christian basics: who God is
- Baptism: belonging to the family of God
- Holy Communion: sharing and caring together

ISBN 978 1 84101 602 3   £8.99
Available from your local Christian bookshop or direct from BRF: visit www.brfonline.org.uk.

Other Messy Church® resources

Messy Church the DVD

Presented by Lucy Moore

Bringing the Messy Church story to life, the DVD is a resource to help those who are thinking of starting a Messy Church to catch the vision, and, for teams already leading a Messy Church, to help develop good practice and inspire further thinking. It features Messy Churches from a variety of situations across the UK, with parents, children, teens and leaders sharing their experiences and wisdom.

The DVD can be used to:

- introduce the concept of Messy Church.
- help a new team understand what starting a Messy Church might entail.
- help an existing team think through some of the important issues faced by leadership teams as the Messy work goes on.

For further resources to help you make best use of the DVD, visit www.messychurch.org.uk/dvd.

ISBN 978 1 84101 849 2   £9.99